JUKE BOX

33 pop songs from the '50s, '60s and '70s

A & C Black · London

First published 1984 by
A & C Black (Publishers) Ltd
35 Bedford Row, London WC1R 4JH
© 1984 A & C Black (Publishers) Ltd
Reprinted 1990

ISBN 0-7136-2402-7

A words only edition (ISBN 0-7136-2401-9) is also available.

Printed in Great Britain by Hollen Street Press Ltd, Slough,
Berkshire

Piano arrangements are by Brian Hunt and Peter Nickol, with
contributions from William Crow (*I'll never fall in love again,
Sealed with a kiss* and *Travellin' light*), Ian Ditchfield (*Bright
eyes, Good morning starshine* and *Poetry in motion*) and Stephen
Firth (*The locomotion*).

Guitar chords and advice on guitar accompaniment by Stewart
Knight.

Cover by Colin Mier

Drawings by Roy Bentley

The songs were chosen by Peter Nickol

Contents

Guitar chords

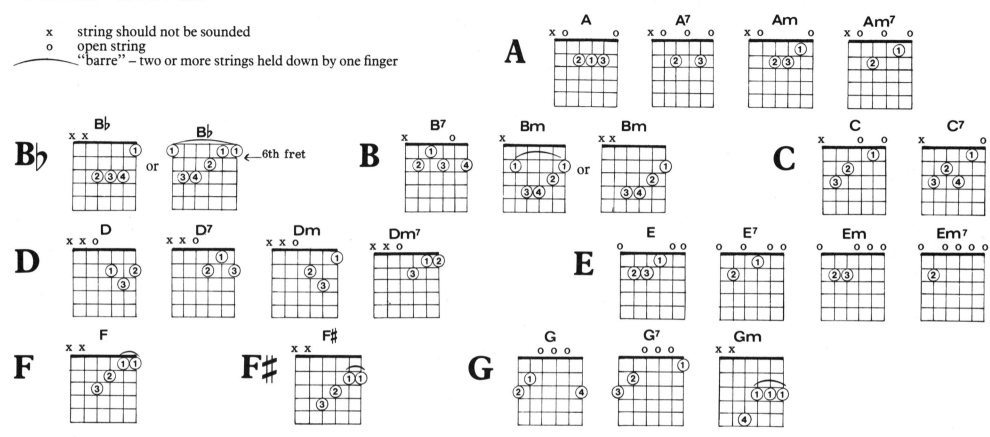

x string should not be sounded
o open string
⌒ "barre" – two or more strings held down by one finger

used in *The windows of the world*

Am add⁹   Fm⁶   C maj⁷

used in *Good morning starshine*

D (bass A)   G⁶ (bass A)

used in *Raining in my heart*

G+

used in *Singing the blues*

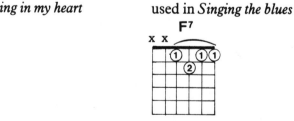

F⁷

used in *There is a happy land*

A⁷ sus   A maj⁷   F add⁹

used in *I can see clearly now*

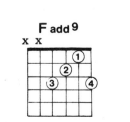

Bm (bass D)   C♯m

used in *I'll never fall in love again*

A♭

Performance and accompaniment

Guitar chord fingerings have as far as possible been chosen for ease of playing. Many chords can be played in a number of different ways, and often the context determines what is best or easiest. For instance in *Sealed with a kiss* the first G major chord should be a barre chord in order to make for an easy change to G minor:

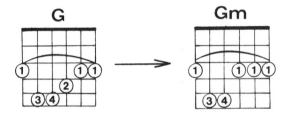

whereas in the bridge section (beginning of line 5) the usual G major fingering can be used. Similarly, in bar 8 of the same song the change from Gm6 to A7 can be fingered like this:

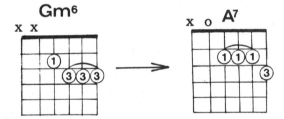

whereas in bar 25 the usual A7 would be used. In *Um um um um um um* a movable barre chord should be used for switching between Gm and Am:

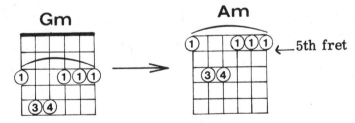

Similarly, in *On Broadway* use barre G and F chords.

In *Singing the blues* the sequence F – F♯ – G is best played with another movable chord shape, using the top four strings only:

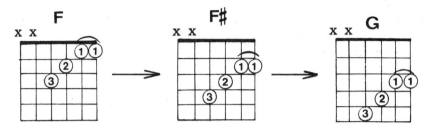

The same shape is much used in reggae rhythms, played staccato by slightly lifting the left hand fingers immediately after playing, damping the strings.

In schools use can be made of existing resources and abilities. With two guitarists, it may be effective to have one playing a bass line, adapted from the chord symbols or from the piano part. Other additions to the instrumentation may be prompted by listening to the original recordings. Triangle or shaker could play the quaver pattern in *Catch a falling star*, and woodblock this rhythm in *Sealed with a kiss*:

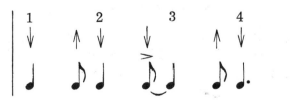

A full pop group line-up, if available, is especially useful in songs like *Book of rules*, where piano alone is inadequate to capture the rhythmic feel of the original.

In *Far far away* an important rhythmic feature of the introduction and the first four bars of each verse is the anticipated 3rd beat. Suggested rhythm guitar strum:

Knowledge of the original recordings should not become stifling; songs can be performed in different ways. Harmony vocals are often effective, and can reduce dependence on instrumental accompaniment. A particular area for initiative is in the treatment of introductions and endings. Songs which were recorded with fade-outs or long codas are here given simple, more-or-less functional endings; these can easily be altered or extended according to taste and available instrumentation.

The piano part, as usual in our song books, has the tune in the right hand. This can beneficially be omitted if the singers are secure. In *All over the world*, for example, the pianist would then be free to play the arpeggios over a wider register, as on the record.

The only song printed here without chord symbols is *Anyone who had a heart*, a marvellous song but very difficult to play on guitar.

Correct notation of many of these songs would involve showing, in small notes, the rhythmic alterations to the melody required by the second and subsequent verses. This sometimes results in very complicated scores, and we have mainly preferred to show only the verse 1 form of the melody. Singers should be aware, therefore, that in certain songs they must adapt the melody when singing the second verse. For instance, verse 2 of *A thing called love* begins:

Most men are like me, they struggle in

doubt, they trouble their minds...

Basically the melody is the same as the first verse, and yet in detail most notes are different. These alterations are purely a practical matter, and can be achieved by recourse to the record or by working out one's own version.

Melodically, too, verse 2 onwards can be treated differently from verse 1. This process can be see in *Um um um um um um*, which is written out in full, but the same principle applies to other songs. In *Book of rules* the Heptones' lead singer not only adapts the rhythm for verse 3 so as to fit the extra syllables, but also alters the melody. Obviously a solo singer has more freedom here than a class or group.

1 On Broadway

Barry Mann/Cynthia Weil/Jerry Leiber/Mike Stoller

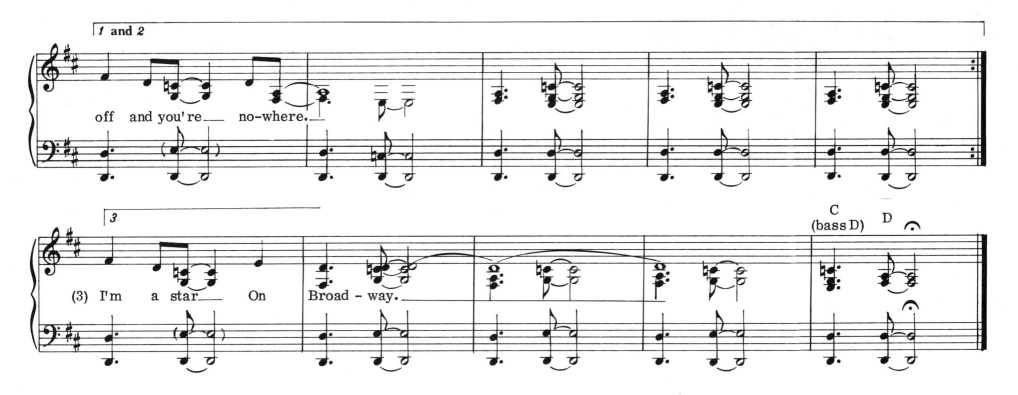

off and you're___ no-where.

(3) I'm a star___ On Broad - way.___

C
(bass D)
D

2   They say the girls are something else
      On Broadway,
   But looking at them just gives me the blues,
   'Cause how you gonna make some time
   When all you got is one thin dime
   And one thin dime won't even shine your shoes.

3   They say that I won't last too long
      On Broadway,
   I'll catch a Greyhound bus for home, they say,
   But they're dead wrong, I know they are,
   'Cause I can play this here guitar
   And I won't quit till I'm a star
      On Broadway.

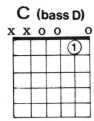

C (bass D)
x x o o

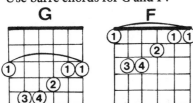

Use barre chords for G and F:
G   F

On the Drifters' record the key is raised a semitone for each new verse.

2 I only want to be with you

Mike Hawker/Ivor Raymonde

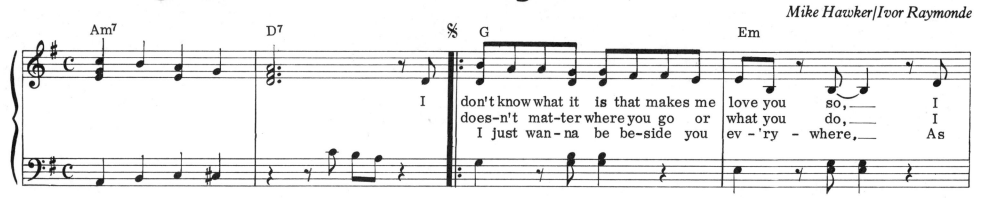

I

I don't know what it is that makes me love you so,___ I
does-n't mat-ter where you go or what you do,___ I
I just wan-na be be-side you ev-'ry - where,___ As

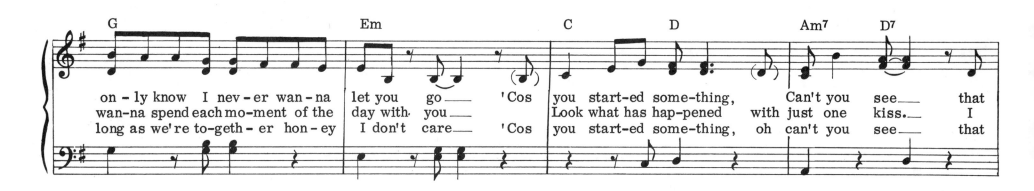

on - ly know I nev-er wan-na let you go___ 'Cos you start-ed some-thing, Can't you see___ that
wan-na spend each mo-ment of the day with you___ Look what has hap-pened with just one kiss.___ I
long as we're to-geth - er hon - ey I don't care___ 'Cos you start-ed some-thing, oh can't you see___ that

3rd time to

ev - er since we met you've had a hold on me.___ It hap - pens to be true.___ I
nev - er knew that I could be in love like this,___ It's cra - zy but it's true.___ I
ev - er since we met you've had a hold on me.___ No mat - ter what you do,___ I

3 The locomotion

Gerry Goffin/Carole King

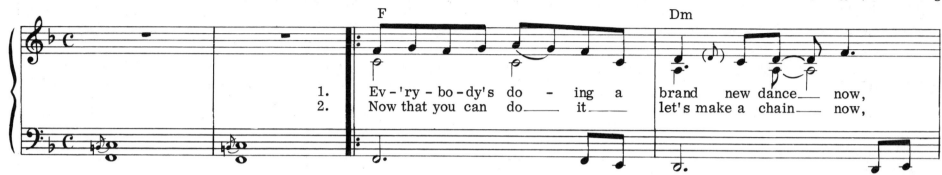

1. Ev-'ry-bo-dy's do - ing a brand new dance now,
2. Now that you can do it let's make a chain now,

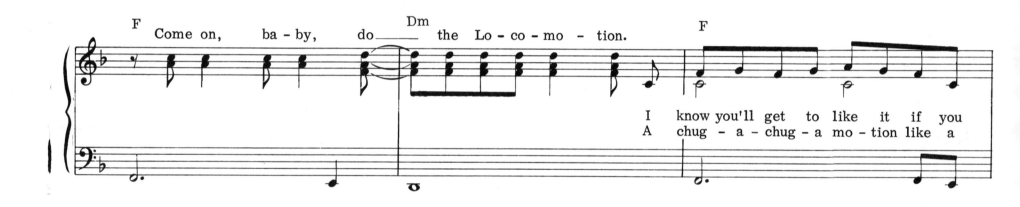

Come on, ba - by, do the Lo - co - mo - tion.

I know you'll get to like it if you
A chug - a - chug - a mo - tion like a

give it a chance now,
rail - road train now,

Come on, ba - by, do the Lo - co - mo - tion.

My

TURN OVER
(*second time*)

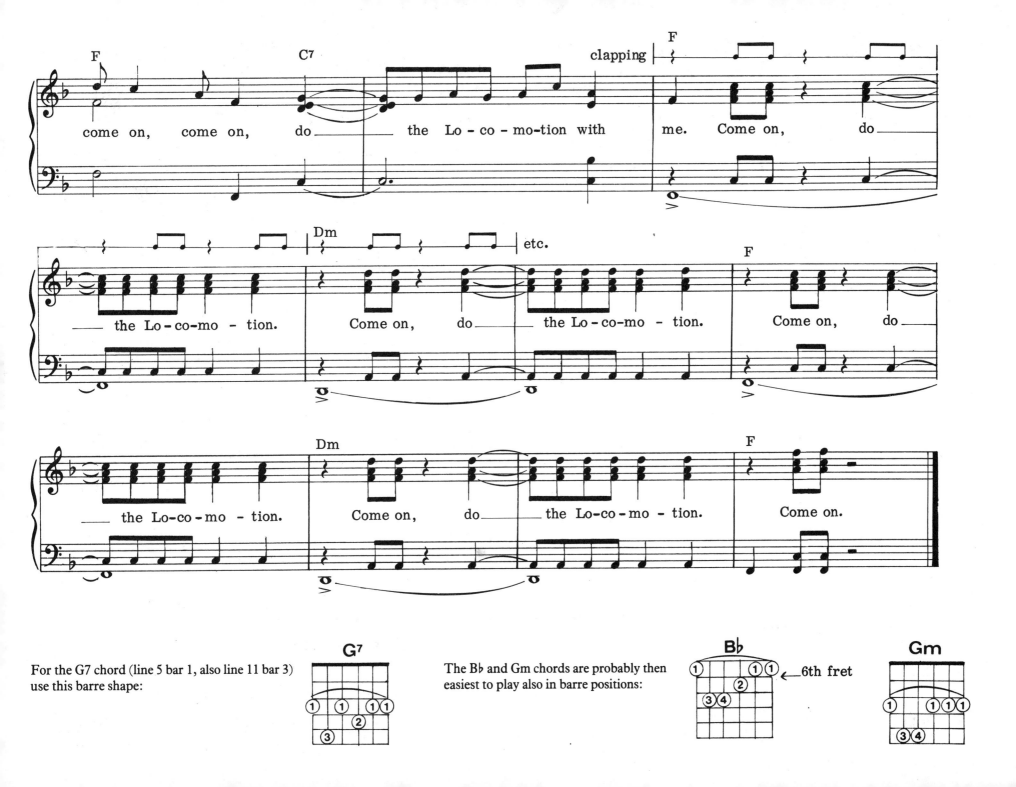

come on, come on, do _____ the Lo-co-mo-tion with me. Come on, do _____

_____ the Lo-co-mo-tion. Come on, do _____ the Lo-co-mo-tion. Come on, do _____

_____ the Lo-co-mo-tion. Come on, do _____ the Lo-co-mo-tion. Come on.

For the G7 chord (line 5 bar 1, also line 11 bar 3) use this barre shape:

The Bb and Gm chords are probably then easiest to play also in barre positions:

4 Moon River

words: Johnny Mercer
music: Henry Mancini

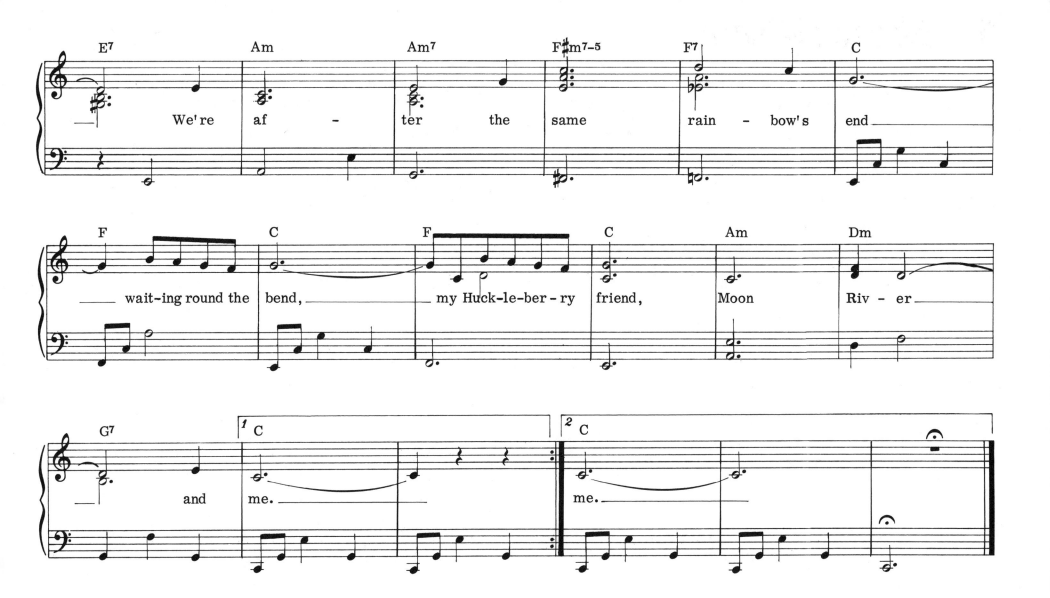

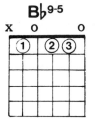
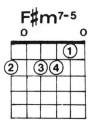
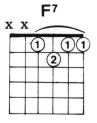

5 Answer me

words: Carl Sigman
music: Gerhard Winkler/Fred Rauch

An-swer me, oh, my love, just what sin have I been guil-ty of?

Tell me how I came to lose your love? Please an-swer me, my love.

You were mine yes-ter-day, I be-lieved that love was here to stay.

Won't you tell me where I've gone a-stray? Please an-swer me, my love.

6 Singing the blues

Melvin Endsley

7 Young love

Carol Joyner/Ric Cartey

8 Allentown Jail

Irving Gordon

1. They've locked up my dar-ling in Al-len-town Jail, Ooh, ooh,____ ooh.

____ And no-one has come forth to put up his bail, Ooh, ooh,____ ooh.

____ They say at the court-house, he'll nev-er go free, Nev - er go

free,____ 'Cause he stole a dia-mond, a beau-ti-ful dia-mond, to give,____ to

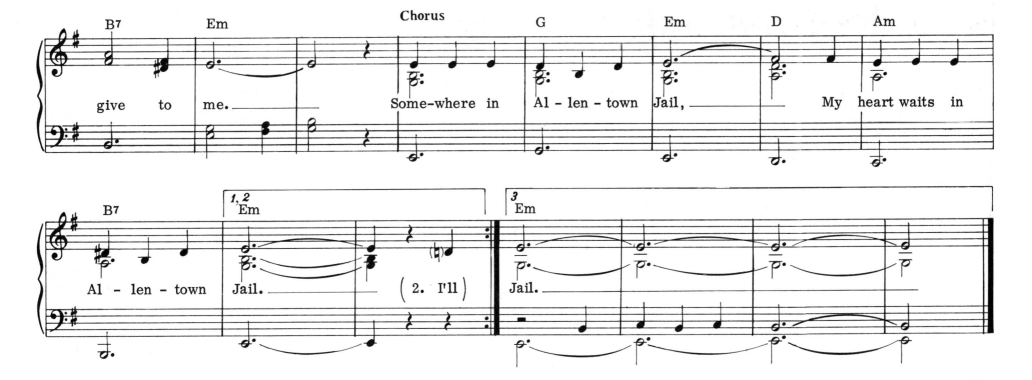

2 I'll dance for you, mister, I'll sing you a song,
    La, da, de, dum.
  But more than that, mister would surely be wrong,
    Mmm, mmm, mmm.
  Oh more than that, mister, would surely be wrong,
  For can't you see,
  My love stole a diamond, a beautiful diamond,
  To give, to give to me.

    Somewhere in Allentown Jail,
    My heart waits in Allentown Jail.

3 You'll find none like him though you search the world round,
    Ooh, ooh, ooh.
  And that's why I'll need the best lawyer in town,
    Ooh, ooh, ooh.
  I must find a lawyer, the best one in town,
  For can't you see.
  My love stole a diamond, a beautiful diamond,
  To prove his love to me.

    Somewhere in Allentown Jail,
    My heart waits in Allentown Jail.

G maj⁷
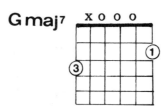

A⁷ sus
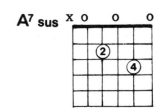

9 Take a message to Mary

Felice Bryant/Boudleaux Bryant

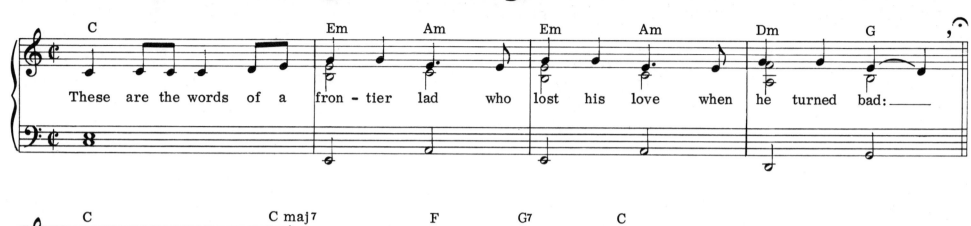

These are the words of a fron - tier lad who lost his love when he turned bad:____

1. Take a mes-sage to Ma - ry   but   don't tell her where I   am,   Take a mes - sage to
2. Take a mes-sage to Ma - ry   but   don't tell her what I've   done,   Please don't men - tion the
3. Take a mes-sage to Ma - ry   but   don't tell her all   you   know,   My heart's ach - ing for

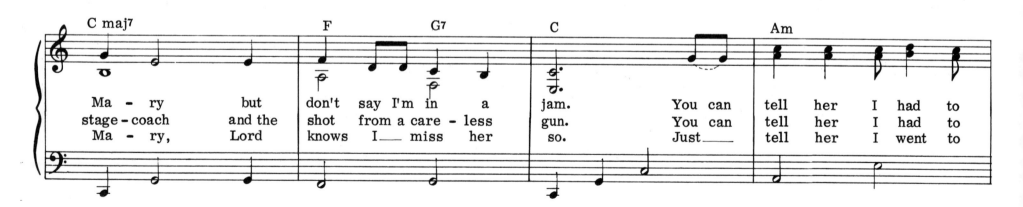

Ma - ry   but   don't   say   I'm in   a   jam.   You can   tell   her   I   had   to
stage - coach   and the   shot   from a care - less   gun.   You can   tell   her   I   had   to
Ma - ry,   Lord   knows   I___ miss   her   so.   Just____   tell   her   I   went   to

see the world,
change my plans and
Tim - buk - tu,

tell her that my ship set
can-cel out the wed - ding
tell her I'm searching for

sail,
day,
gold,

You can
But
You can

say she'd bet - ter not
please don't men-tion my
say she'd bet - ter find

wait for me but
lone - ly cell where
some - one new to

don't tell her I'm in
I'm gon-na pine a -
cher-ish and to

jail,
way
hold.

oh,
un - til
Oh

don't tell her I'm in
my dy - ing
Lord this cell is

jail.
day.
cold.

quietly

Ma - ry, Ma - ry, Oh Lord this cell is cold.

C maj⁷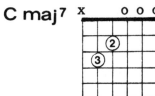

10 Poetry in motion

Paul Kaufman/Mike Anthony

11 Sealed with a kiss

words: Peter Udell
music: Gary Geld

12 It might as well rain until September

Gerry Goffin/Carole King

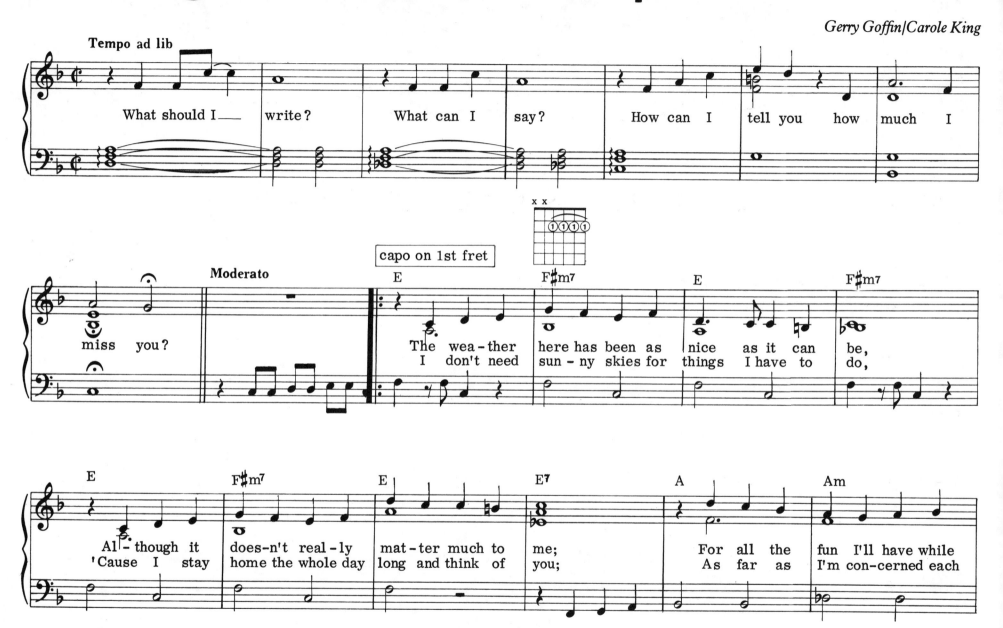

What should I — write? What can I say? How can I tell you how much I

miss you? The wea-ther here has been as nice as it can be,
I don't need sun-ny skies for things I have to do,

Al-though it does-n't real-ly mat-ter much to me; For all the fun I'll have while
'Cause I stay home the whole day long and think of you; As far as I'm con-cerned each

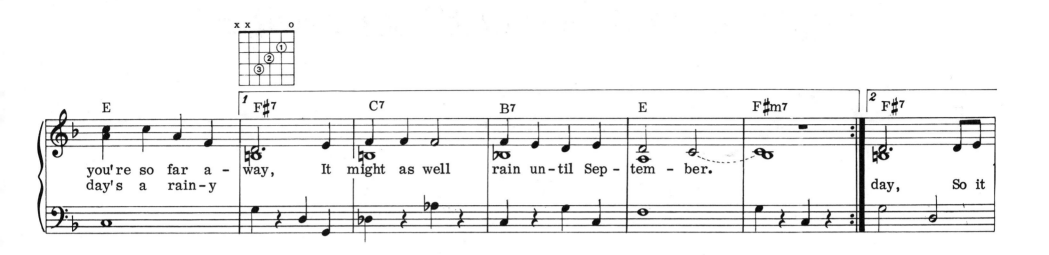

TURN OVER

13 Travellin' light

Sid Tepper/Roy C. Bennett

Got no bags and baggage to slow me down,_____ I'm

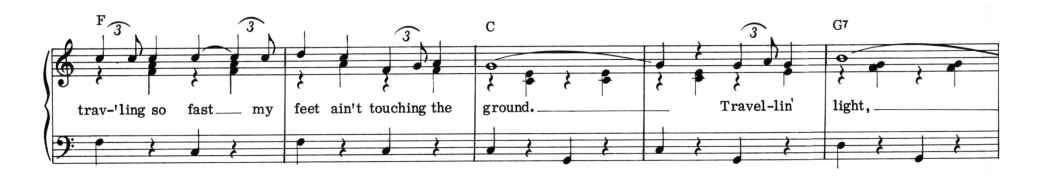

trav-'ling so fast___ my feet ain't touching the ground._____ Travel-lin' light,_____

____ travel-lin' light,_____ Well I just can't wait___ to be with my ba-by to-night.

TURN OVER

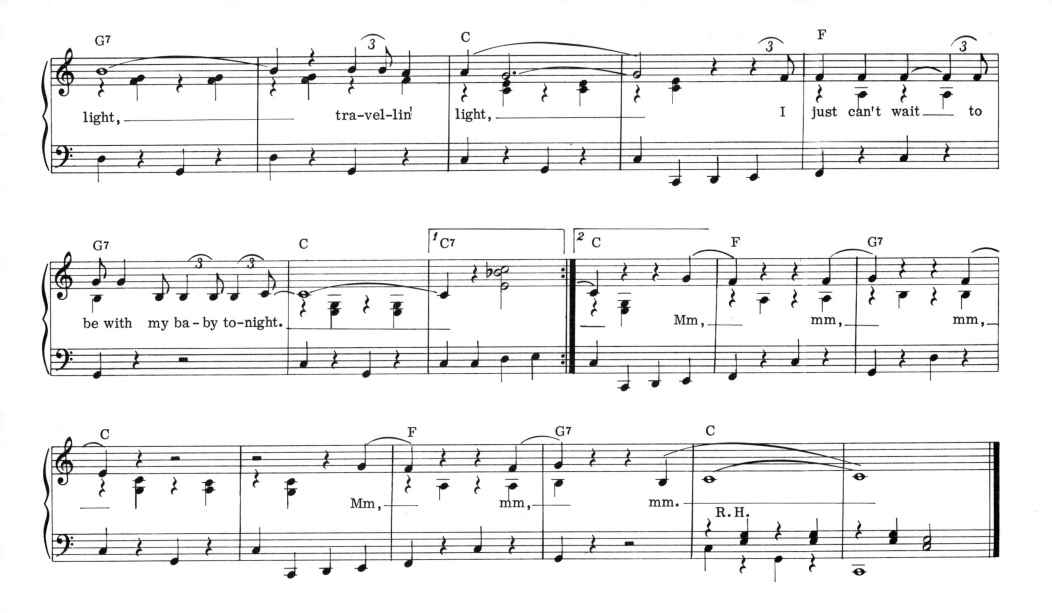

light, _____ tra-vel-lin' light, _____ I just can't wait _____ to be with my ba-by to-night. Mm, ____ mm, ____ mm, ____ Mm, ____ mm, ____ mm. _____

Guitar

There's an "um-cha" effect characteristic of this type of song. Play bass notes on the 1st and 3rd beats, and chords (using the top three strings) on the 2nd and 4th beats. The bass line mostly alternates between the root and fifth of the chord. As in the piano part, it is effective to break this pattern at certain points, e.g. at bar 16 ("be with my baby tonight") and bars 25–28 ("pocket full of dreams . . .").

14 Raining in my heart

Boudleaux Bryant/Felice Bryant

The sun is out,— the sky is blue,— there's not a cloud— to spoil the view— but it's rain-ing, rain-ing in my heart.

The weath-er-man— says "Clear to-day,"— he does-n't know— you've gone a-way— and it's rain-ing, rain-ing in my heart.

Oh mis-e-

15 Book of rules

Guitar

For a reggae effect, play very staccato on the 2nd and 4th beats, using only the top three or four strings, movable chord shape, no open strings: Damp the strings just after playing by releasing the left hand finger pressure slightly.

Perform sections in this order: intro – A(verse 1) – B – A(verse 2) – B – C – B – A(verse 3) – B – C

H. Johnson/B. Llewelwyn

1. Is-n't it strange how prin-ces-ses and
2. Each must make his life as flow-ing
3. Look when the rain has fal-len from the

kings
in,
sky,

(v.3: ♪ ♩ ♪ | ♩ etc.)

dance clowns' rag-ged ca-pers in the saw-dust ring.
tumb-ling back___ on a step-ping stone.
I know the sun will be on-ly mis-sing for a while.

Just like all the peo-ple like you and me, we'll be buil-ders for e-ter-ni-ty.___

16 Up on the roof

Gerry Goffin/Carole King

1. When this old world starts
(2) tir - ed and beat
(3) (starts instrumental- - -

get-ting me down and
I
-

peo-ple are just too much for me to face___
go up where the air is fresh and sweet.___
(verse 3 starts instrumental; voice resumes at bottom of page - - - - - - - -

I climb way up to the
I get a - way from the

top of the stairs and all my cares just drift right in - to space.___
hus-tl-ing crowds and all that rat - race noise down in the street.___

At

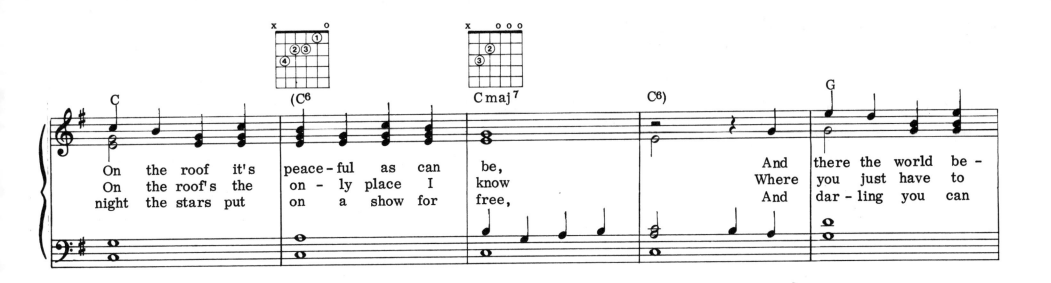

On the roof it's peace-ful as can be,
On the roof's the on-ly place I know
night the stars put on a show for

And there the world be-
be, Where you just have to
free, And dar-ling you can

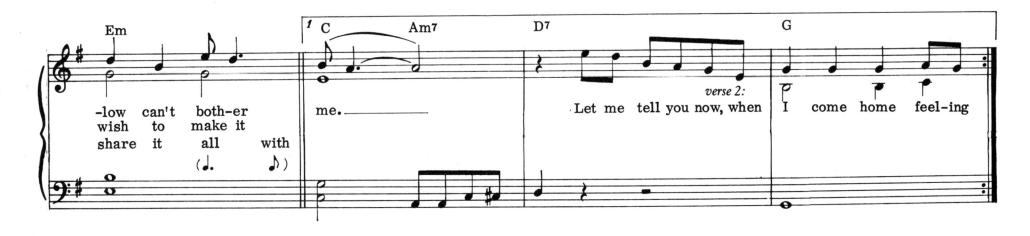

-low can't both-er me.
wish to make it
share it all with

Let me tell you now, when I come home feel-ing

verse 2:

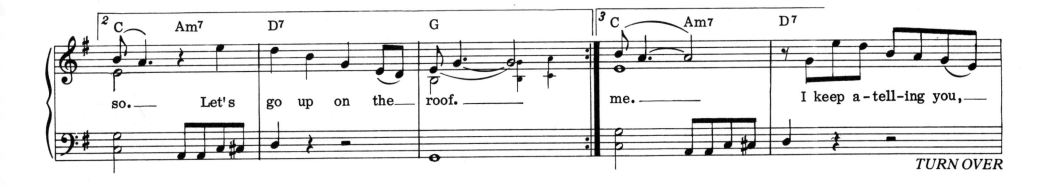

so. Let's go up on the roof.

me.

I keep a-tell-ing you,

TURN OVER

17 Um, um, um, um, um, um

Curtis Mayfield

through the park,—— it wasn't quite dark, there was a man sit-ting on a bench.——
(simile)

Out of the crowd,—with his head—— low-ly bowed,— he'd just moan and it made no sense,—— he'd just go:

Um, um um um um, um, um um um um um.——

TURN OVER
(*second time*)

18 Falling in love again

words: Reg Connelly
music: Friederich Holländer

Falling in love again,
Never wanted to,
What am I to do,
I can't help it.

Love's always been my game,
Play it how I may,
I was made that way,
I can't help it.

    Men cluster to me
    Like moths around a flame,
    And if their wings burn
    I know I'm not to blame,

I'm falling in love again,
Never wanted to,
What am I to do,
I can't help it.

D+

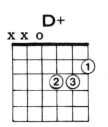

The guitar and piano parts are not compatible, as they are
different harmonisations.

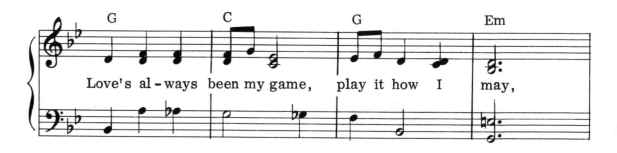

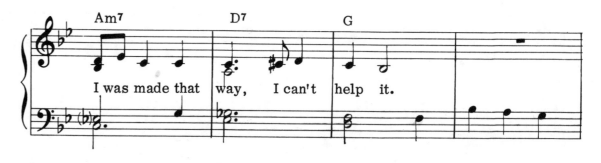

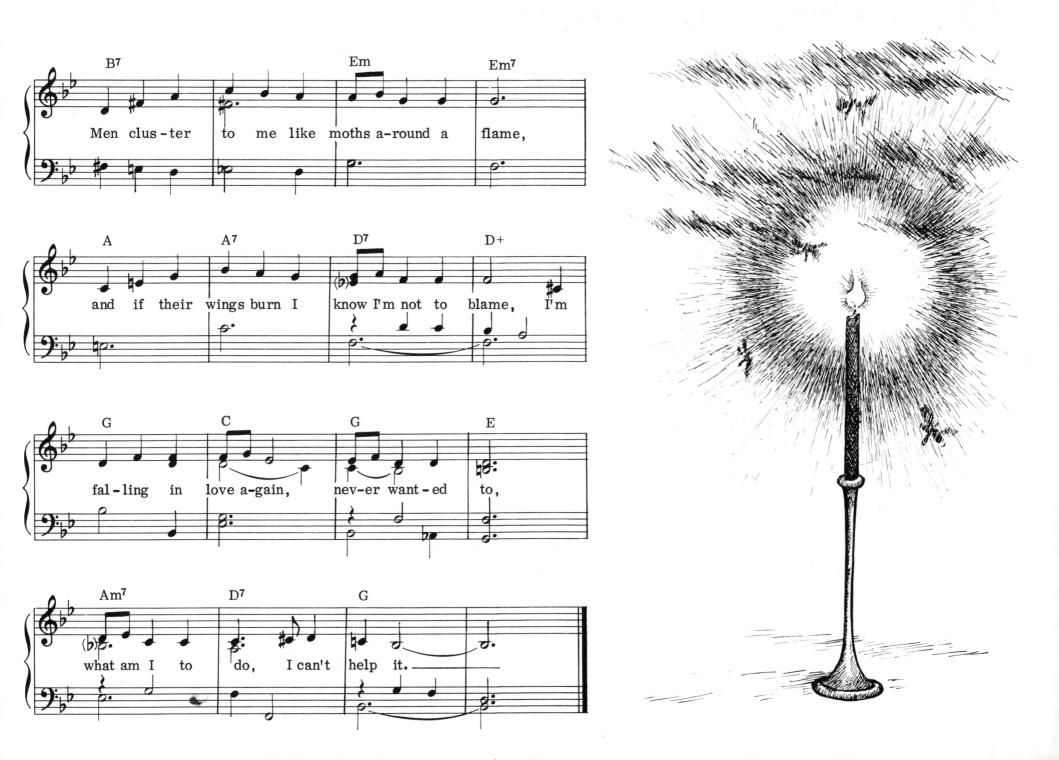

19 Anyone who had a heart

words: Hal David
music: Burt Bacharach

20 The windows of the world

words: Hal David
music: Burt Bacharach

1 The windows of the world are covered with rain.
Where is the sunshine we once knew?
   Everybody knows
   when little childen play
   they need a sunny day
   to grow straight and tall.
Let the sun shine through.

2 The windows of the world are covered with rain.
When will those black skies turn to blue?
   Everybody knows
   when boys grow into men
   they start to wonder when
   their country will call.
Let the sun shine through.

3 The windows of the world are covered with rain.
What is the whole world coming to?
   Everybody knows
   when men cannot be friends
   their quarrel often ends
   where some have to die.
Let the sun shine through.

4 The windows of the world are covered with rain.
There must be something we can do.
   Everybody knows
   whenever rain appears
   it's really angel tears.
   How long must they cry?
Let the sun shine through.

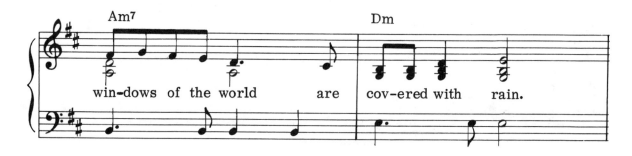

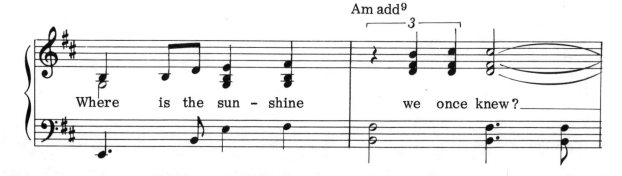

21 Good morning starshine

words: James Rado/Gerome Ragni
music: Galt MacDermot

22 All over the world

23 Dedicated follower of fashion

Raymond Douglas Davies

They seek him here

they seek him there, ___
his lit-tle rounds, ___
they seek him there, ___

His clothes are loud
Round the Bou-tiques
In Re-gent Street ___

but nev-er square
of Lon-don Town
and Leicester Square

It will make or break him so he's
Ea-ger-ly pur-su-ing all the
Ev-'ry-where the Carn-a-by-tian

got to buy the best, 'cos he's a
la-test fads and trends, 'cos he's a
ar-my march-es on, Each one a

TURN OVER

There's | one thing that he loves, and that is | flat-te-ry, | | One week he's in
He | flits from shop to shop just like a | but-ter-fly, | | In mat-ters of the

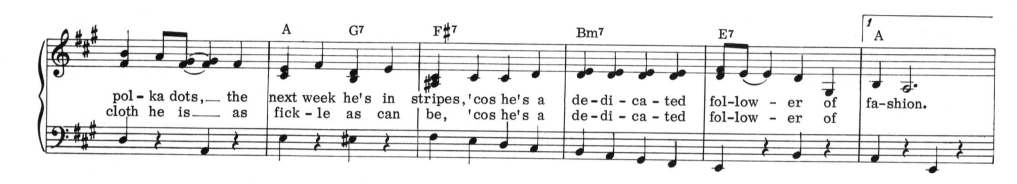

pol - ka dots,— the | next week he's in stripes,'cos he's a | de-di-ca-ted | fol-low - er of | fa-shion.
cloth he is— as | fick - le as can be, 'cos he's a | de-di-ca-ted | fol-low - er of |

D.S.
(without repeat)
They seek him—here

TURN BACK

fa - shion. | He's a | de - di - ca - ted | fol-low-er of

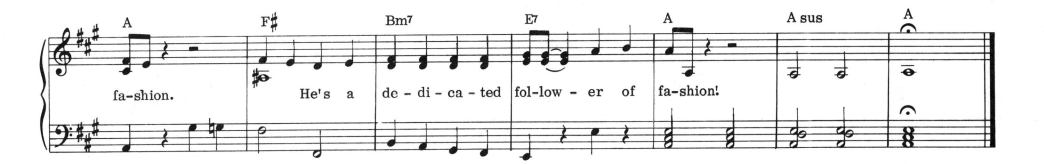

fa-shion.   He's a de - di - ca - ted fol-low - er of fa-shion!

They seek him here, they seek him there,
His clothes are loud, but never square.
It will make or break him so he's got to buy the best,
'Cos he's a dedicated follower of fashion.

And when he does his little rounds
Round the boutiques of London Town
Eagerly pursuing all the latest fads and trends,
'Cos he's a dedicated follower of fashion.

 Oh yes he is! (Oh yes he is!)
 Oh yes he is! (Oh yes he is!)

He thinks he is a flower to be looked at,
And when he pulls his frilly nylon panties right up tight
He feels a dedicated follower of fashion.
 Oh yes he is! (Oh yes he is!) . . .

There's one thing that he loves and that is flattery,
One week he's in polka dots, the next week he's in stripes,
'Cos he's a dedicated follower of fashion.

They seek him here, they seek him there,
In Regent Street and Leicester Square.
Ev'rywhere the Carnabytian army marches on,
Each one a dedicated follower of fashion.
 Oh yes he is! (Oh yes he is!) . . .

His world is built round discotheques and parties,
This pleasure-seeking individual always looks
 his best,
'Cos he's a dedicated follower of fashion.
 Oh yes he is! (Oh yes he is!) . . .

He flits from shop to shop just like a butterfly.
In matters of the cloth he is as fickle as can be,
'Cos he's a dedicated follower of fashion,
He's a dedicated follower of fashion,
He's a dedicated follower of fashion!

Guitar
Strum with the general feel of this rhythm:

24   I'll never fall in love again

words: Hal David
music: Burt Bacharach

25 Catch a falling star

Paul Vance/Lee Pockriss

shaker etc.

C

Catch a fal-ling star and
put it in your pock-et, Never let it fade a - way. Catch a fal-ling star and put it in your pock-et,

Save it for a rain-y day. For

F   C

love may come and tap___ you on the shoulder,   Some star-less
when your trou-bles start___ in mul-ti-ply - ing,   And they just

night.   And   C tacet
might,   It's

F

just in case you feel___ you want to hold her,   You'll have a pock - et full of star-light.
ea - sy to for-get___ them without try - ing,   With just a pock - et full of star-light.

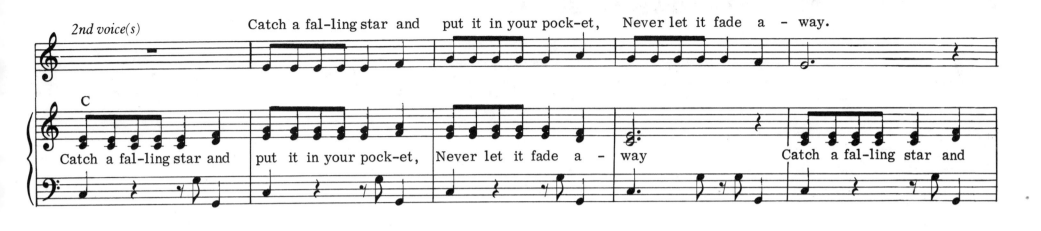

2nd voice(s) Catch a fal-ling star and put it in your pock-et, Never let it fade a - way.

C

Catch a fal-ling star and put it in your pock-et, Never let it fade a - way Catch a fal-ling star and

Catch a falling star and put it in your pock-et, Save it for a rain-y **1** day. **2** day.

put it in your pock-et, Save it for a rain-y day. For Save it for a rain-y

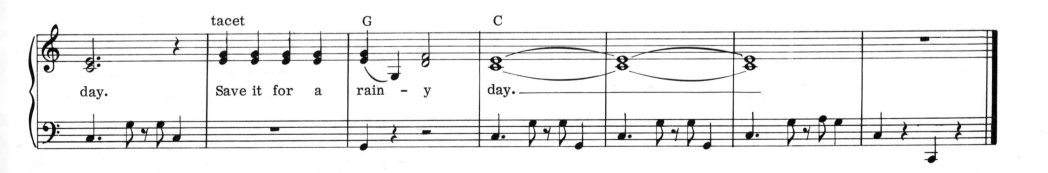

tacet G C

day. Save it for a rain - y day.

26 There is a happy land

David Bowie

27 A thing called love

Jerry Hubbard

1. Six foot six he stood on the ground,— he weighed two hundred and thirty-five pounds, but I saw that

gi-ant of a man brought down to his knees by love. He was a kind of a man that would gamble on

love, look you in the eye and nev-er back up, But I saw him crying like a lit-tle whipped pup because of

love. You can't see it with your eyes, hold it in your hand, but like the wind it covers our

land: Strong enough to rule the heart of an-y man,— this thing called love.

It can lift you up, ne-ver let you down, take your world and turn it all a - round.— E-ver since

time nothing's ev-er been found that's stronger than love. 2. Most men are like Ev-er since

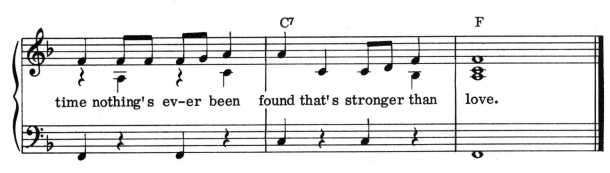

time nothing's ev-er been found that's stronger than love.

2 Most men are like me, they struggle in doubt,
  They trouble their minds day in and day out,
  Too busy with living to worry about
    a little word like love.
  But when I see a mother's tenderness
  As she holds her young close to her breast,
  Then I thank God that the world's been blessed
    with a thing called love.
      You can't see it with your eyes . . .

28   I can see clearly now

Johnny Nash

capo on 3rd fret

1. & 3.   I can see clear - ly now, ___ the rain
2.   I think I can make ___ it now, ___ the pain

___ has gone. ___   I can see all ___ ob - stac - les   in my way.
___ has gone. ___   All of the bad ___ feel - ings have   dis-ap-peared.

Gone are the dark ___ clouds that had me blind, _   It's gon-na be a
Here is the rain - bow I've been pray-ing for, _

bright,   bright sun-shi-ny day, ___   It's gon-na be a   bright,

29 Bright eyes

Mike Batt

1. Is it a kind of dream floating out on the tide,
2. Is it a kind of sha - dow reaching in - to the night,

fol-low-ing the ri-ver of death down-stream oh is it a dream? There's a
wan-der ing o - ver the hills un - seen or is it a dream? There's a

fog a-long the hor - i - zon, a strange glow in the sky, and
high wind in the trees, a cold sound in the air, and

30 Chirpy chirpy cheep cheep

Lally Stott

31 Far far away

James Lea/Neville Holder

3 I've seen the Paris lights from high upon Montmartre
   And felt the silence hanging low in no man's land;
   And all those Spanish nights were fine,
   It wasn't only from the wine;
   It still seems all in hand.
        And I'm far, far away . . .

4 I've seen the yellow lights go down the Mississippi,
   The grand Bahama island stories carry on;
   And all those funny kinda smiles
   Stay in your memory for a while;
   There still seems more to come.
        And I'm far, far away . . .

32 The rainbow connection

Paul Williams/Kenny Ascher

1 Why are there so many songs about rainbows,
And what's on the other side?
Rainbows are visions, but only illusions,
And rainbows have nothing to hide.
    So we've been told, and some choose to believe it;
    I know they're wrong; wait and see.
Someday we'll find it, the rainbow connection;
The lovers, the dreamers, and me.

2 Who said that every wish would be heard and answered
When wished on the morning star?
Somebody thought of that, and someone believed it;
Look what it's done so far.
    What's so amazing that keeps us star-gazing
    And what do we think we might see?
Someday we'll find it, the rainbow connection;
The lovers, the dreamers, and me.

3 Have you been half-asleep and have you heard voices?
I've heard them calling my name.
Is this the sweet sound that calls the young sailors?
The voice might be one and the same.
    I've heard it too many times to ignore it.
    It's something that I'm s'posed to be.
Someday we'll find it, the rainbow connection;
The lovers, the dreamers, and me.

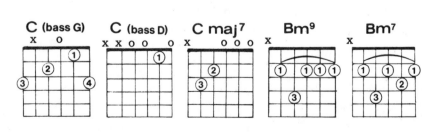

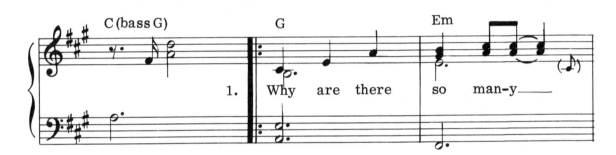

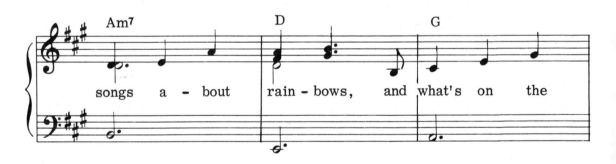

33   I love you because

Leon Payne

al - ways see me through._____ I love you for the way you ne - ver
al - ways be true._____ I love you for a hun - dred thou - sand

doubt me,_____ But most of all I love you 'cause you're you._____
rea - sons,_____ But most of all I love you 'cause you're you._____

1 I love you because you understand, dear,
   Ev'ry single thing I try to do.
   You're always there to lend a helping hand, dear,
   I love you most of all because you're you.
   No matter what the world may say about me,
   I know your love will always see me through.
   I love you for the way you never doubt me,
   But most of all I love you 'cause you're you.

2 I love you because my heart is lighter
   Ev'ry time I'm walking by your side.
   I love you because the future's brighter.
   The door to happiness you open wide.
   No matter what may be the style or season,
   I know your heart will always be true.
   I love you for a hundred thousand reasons,
   But most of all I love you 'cause you're you.

Acknowledgements

The publishers would like to thank Stewart Knight for his invaluable help with guitar chords.

The following copyright owners have kindly granted their permission for the reprinting of words and music:

Editions Musicales Alpha for 22 "All over the world".

Barn Publishing (Slade) Ltd for 31 "Far far away".

Bourne Music Ltd for 8 "Allentown Jail"; with Acuff-Rose Publications Pty Ltd for 33 "I love you because"; and with Papageno-Verlag Dr Hans Sikorski for 5 "Answer me".

Campbell Connelly & Co Ltd, 37 Soho Square, London W1V 5DG, for 18 "Falling in love again" © 1930 Ufa-Musikverlage, Munich, West Germany.

Carlin Music Corporation: with Castle Music Pty Ltd and Intersong Pty Ltd for 19 "Anyone who had a heart" and 23 "Dedicated follower of fashion"; with Chappell Music (Australia) and Intersong Pty Ltd for 13 "Travellin' light"; and with Jonathan Music (Australia) Pty Ltd for 20 "The windows of the world" and 24 "I'll never fall in love again".

CPP/Belwin Inc and International Music Publications for 11 "Sealed with a kiss" © 1960 United Artists Music Co Inc, and 21 "Good morning starshine" © 1966, 1967, 1968 James Rado, Galt MacDermot, Nat Shapiro, Jerome Ragni and United Artists Music Co Ltd.

EMI Music Publishing Ltd and International Music Publications for 25 "Catch a falling star" © 1957 Marvin Music Co, 3 "The Locomotion", 12 "It might as well rain until September" and 16 "Up on the roof", all © 1962 Screen Gems/EMI Music Inc, and for 32 "The rainbow connection" © 1979 Welbeck Music Corp.

EMI Songs Ltd and International Music Publications for 29 "Bright Eyes" © 1978 EMI Songs Ltd.

Intersong Music Ltd and International Music Publications for 30 "Chirpy chirpy cheep cheep".

Island Music for 15 "Book of rules".

MCA Music Ltd for 27 "A thing called love" © 1968, 1970 Vector Music Corp, Valley Music Ltd for British Commonwealth (excl Canada & Australasia) and South Africa.

Ivan Mogull Music Corporation for 17 "Um um um um um um".

Music Sales Ltd for 6 "Singing the blues" © 1954 Acuff Rose Publications Inc, 9 "Take a message to Mary" © 1959 Acuff Rose Publications Inc, and 14 "Raining in my heart" © 1959 Acuff Rose Publications Inc.

The Sparta Florida Music Group Ltd for 26 "There is a happy land".

Warner Chappell Music Ltd and International Music Publications for 2 "I only want to be with you" © 1963 Chappell & Co Ltd, 4 "Moon River" © 1961 Famous Music Corp, 10 "Poetry in motion" © 1960 Vogue Music Corp, and 28 "I can see clearly now".

TRO Essex Music Ltd and Essex Music of Australia Pty Ltd for 7 "Young love" © 1957 and 1973 Lowery Music Inc, assigned to Cromwell Music Ltd for the world excl USA Canada Australasia Germany Austria Switzerland Norway Sweden Denmark Finland Iceland and Mexico; international copyright secured; all rights reserved.

Every effort has been made to trace and acknowledge copyright owners. If any right has been omitted, the publishers offer their apologies and will rectify this in subsequent editions following notification.

Index of first lines